Meat Loaf
BAT OUT OF HELL

Songs by
JIM STEINMAN

As recorded on the Epic/Cleveland International Record Album "Bat Out of Hell".

Contents

Piano arrangements by Frank Metis

Cover Concept: Jim Steinman
Illustration: Richard Corben
Cover Design: Ed Lee
Photographs: Frank Laffitte and D. Hunstein

ISBN 978-0-7935-0765-8

EDWARD B.
MARKS MUSIC
COMPANY

EXCLUSIVELY DISTRIBUTED BY

HAL•LEONARD®
CORPORATION
7777 W. BLUEMOUND RD. P.O. BOX 13819 MILWAUKEE, WI 53213

BAT OUT OF HELL

Words and Music by
JIM STEINMAN

The sirens are screaming and the fires are howling
Way down in the valley tonight
There's a man in the shadows with a gun in his eye
And a blade shining oh so bright
There's evil in the air and there's thunder in the sky
And a killer's on the bloodshot streets
And down in the tunnel where the deadly are rising
Oh I swear I saw a young boy
Down in the gutter
He was starting to foam in the heat

Oh Baby you're the only thing in this whole world
        that's pure and good and right
And wherever you are and wherever you go
There's always gonna be some light
But I gotta get out
I gotta break it out now
Before the final crack of dawn
So we gotta make the most of our one night together
When it's over you know
We'll both be so alone

Like a bat out of hell
I'll be gone when the morning comes
When the night is over
Like a bat out of hell I'll be gone gone gone
Like a bat out of hell I'll be gone when the morning comes
But when the day is done
And the sun goes down
And the moonlight's shining through
Then like a sinner before the gates of heaven
I'll come crawling on back to you

I'm gonna hit the highway like a battering ram
On a silver black phantom bike
When the metal is hot and the engine is hungry
And we're all about to see the light
Nothing ever grows in this rotting old hole
Everything is stunted and lost
And nothing really rocks
And nothing really rolls
And nothing's ever worth the cost
And I know that I'm damned if I never get out
And maybe I'm damned if I do
But with every other beat I got left in my heart
You know I'd rather be damned with you
If I gotta be damned you know I wanna be damned
Dancing through the night with you
If I gotta be damned you know I wanna be damned
Gotta be damned you know I wanna be damned
If I gotta be damned you know I wanna be damned
Dancing through the night
Dancing through the night
Dancing through the night with you

Oh Baby you're the only thing in this whole world
        that's pure and good and right
And wherever you are and wherever you go
There's always gonna be some light
But I gotta get out
I gotta break it out now
Before the final crack of dawn
So we gotta make the most of our one night together
When it's over you know
We'll both be so alone

Like a bat out of hell
I'll be gone when the morning comes
When the night is over
Like a bat out of hell I'll be gone gone gone
Like a bat out of hell I'll be gone when the morning comes
But when the day is done
And the sun goes down
And the moonlight's shining through
Then like a sinner before the gates of heaven
I'll come crawling on back to you
Then like a sinner before the gates of heaven
I'll come crawling on back to you

I can see myself tearing up the road
Faster than any other boy has ever gone
And my skin is raw but my soul is ripe
No one's gonna stop me now
I gotta make my escape

But I can't stop thinking of you
And I never see the sudden curve until it's way too late
I never see the sudden curve till it's way too late

Then I'm dying at the bottom of a pit in the blazing sun
Torn and twisted at the foot of a burning bike
And I think somebody somewhere must be tolling a bell
And the last thing I see is my heart
Still beating
Breaking out of my body
And flying away
Like a bat out of hell
Then I'm dying at the bottom of a pit in the blazing sun
Torn and twisted at the foot of a burning bike
And I think somebody somewhere must be tolling a bell
And the last thing I see is my heart
Still beating
Still beating
Breaking out of my body and flying away
Like a bat out of hell
Like a bat out of hell
Like a bat out of hell
Like a bat out of hell
Like a bat out of hell
Like a bat out of hell

BAT OUT OF HELL

Words and Music by
JIM STEINMAN

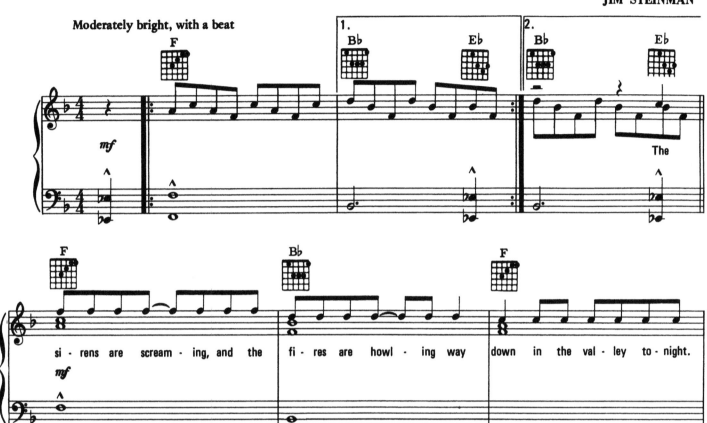

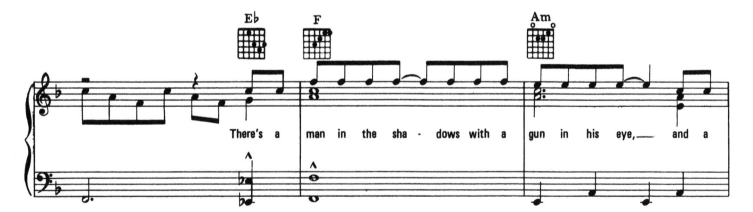

right. And wher-ev-er you are,___ and wher-ev-er you go,___ there's

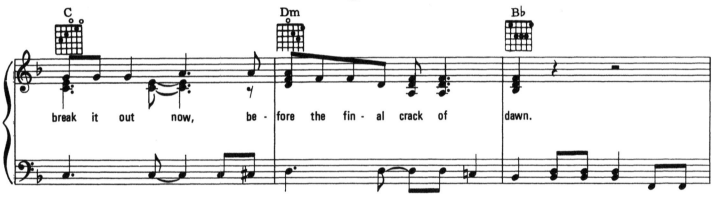

al-ways gon-na be some light. But I got-ta get out,___ I got-ta

break it out now, be-fore the fin-al crack of dawn.

So we got-ta make the most of our one night to-geth-er, when it's

o-ver you know,___ we'll both be so a-lone.___

poco a poco cresc.

Like a

Bat Out Of Hell,___ I'll be gone___ when the morn - ing comes.___

f

When the night is o - ver, like a Bat Out Of Hell,___ I'll be

gone, gone,___ gone.

Like a Bat Out Of Hell,___ I'll be gone___

___ when the morn - ing comes.

But when the

an- y oth-er boy has ev - er gone.

And my skin is raw____. but my

soul is ripe,____ and no one's gon-na stop me now,____ I'm gon-na make____ my es-

cape! But I can't stop think-ing of you,____

And I nev-er see the sud-den curve____ till it's way too

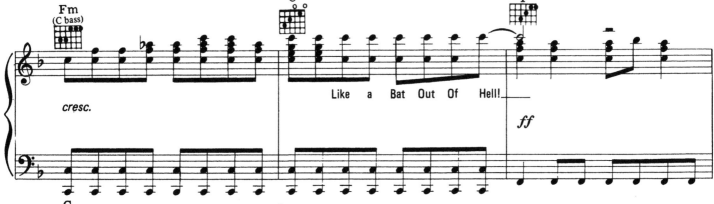

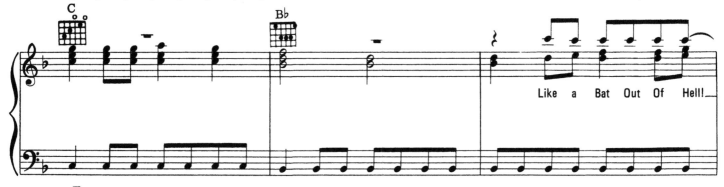

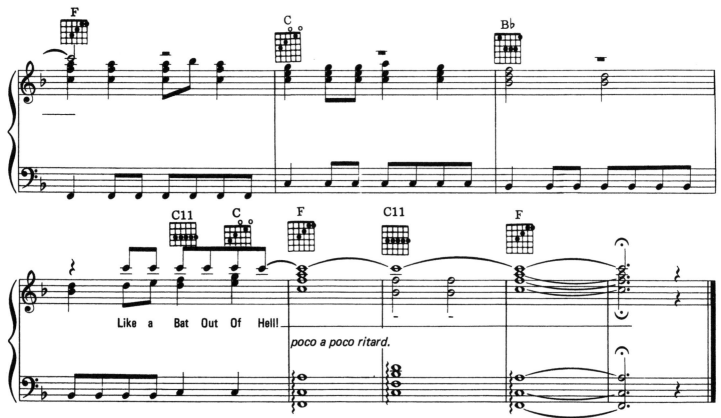

BOY: On a hot summer night would you offer your throat to the wolf with the red roses?
GIRL: Will he offer me his mouth?
BOY: Yes
GIRL: Will he offer me his teeth?
BOY: Yes
GIRL: Will he offer me his jaws?
BOY: Yes
GIRL: Will he offer me his hunger?
BOY: Yes
GIRL: And will he starve without me?
BOY: Yes
GIRL: Then does he love me?
BOY: Yes
GIRL: Yes
BOY: On a hot summer night would you offer your throat to the wolf with the red roses?
GIRL: Yes
BOY: I bet you say that to all the boys.

YOU TOOK THE WORDS RIGHT OUT OF MY MOUTH
(Hot Summer Night)
Words and Music by
JIM STEINMAN

It was a hot summer night and the beach was burning
There was fog crawling over the sand
When I listen to your heart I hear the whole world turning
I see the shooting stars
Falling through your trembling hands

You were licking your lips and your lipstick shining
I was dying just to ask for a taste
We were lying together in a silver lining
By the light of the moon
You know there's not another moment
Not another moment
Not another moment to waste

You hold me so close that my knees grow weak
But my soul is flying high above the ground
I'm trying to speak but no matter what I do
I just can't seem to make any sound

And then you took the words right out of my mouth
Oh—it must have been while you were kissing me
You took the words right out of my mouth
And I swear it's true
I was just about to say I love you
And then you took the words right out of my mouth
Oh—it must have been while you were kissing me
You took the words right out of my mouth
And I swear it's true
I was just about to say I love you

Now my body is shaking like a wave on the water
And I guess that I'm beginning to grin
Oooh, we're finally alone and we can do what we want to
The night is young
And ain't no one gonna know where you
No one gonna know where you
No one's gonna know where you've been

You were licking your lips and your lipstick shining
I was dying just to ask for a taste
We were lying together in a silver lining
By the light of the moon
You know there's not another moment
Not another moment
Not another moment to waste

And then you took the words right out of my mouth
Oh—it must have been while you were kissing me
You took the words right out of my mouth
And I swear it's true
I was just about to say I love you
And then you took the words right out of my mouth
Oh—it must have been while you were kissing me
You took the words right out of my mouth
And I swear it's true
I was just about to say I love you

YOU TOOK THE WORDS RIGHT OUT OF MY MOUTH
(Hot Summer Night)

Words and Music by
JIM STEINMAN

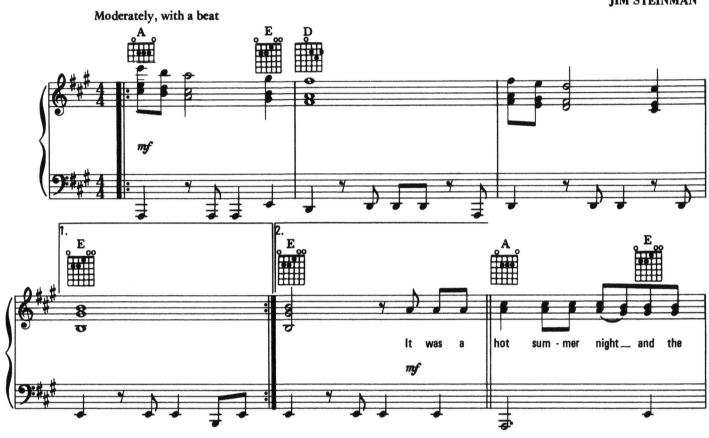

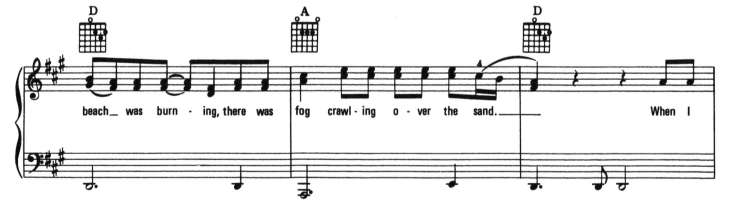

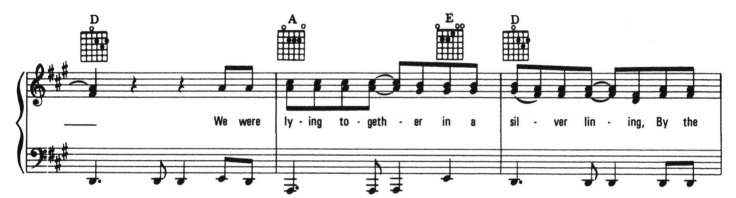

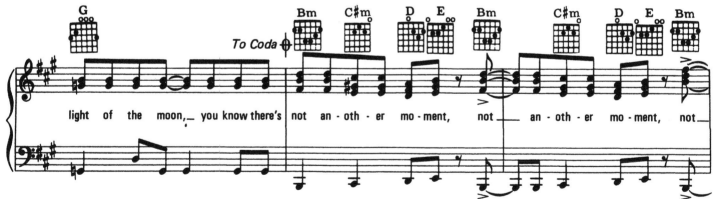

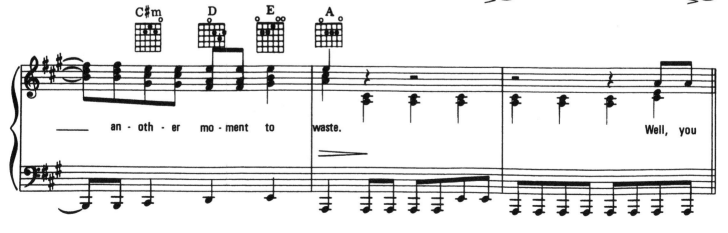

D. S. al Coda

JIM STEINMAN

HEAVEN CAN WAIT

Words and Music by
JIM STEINMAN

Heaven can wait
And a band of angels wrapped up in my heart
Will take me through the lonely night
Through the cold of the day
And I know
I know
Heaven can wait
And all the gods come down here just to sing for me
And the melody's gonna make me fly
Without pain
Without fear

Give me all of your dreams
And let me go along on your way
Give me all of your prayers to sing
And I'll turn the night into the skylight of day
I got a taste of paradise
I'm never gonna let it slip away
I got a taste of paradise
It's all I really need to make me stay—
Just like a child again

Heaven can wait
And all I got is time until the end of time
I won't look back
I won't look back
Let the altars shine

And I know that I've been released
But I don't know to where
And nobody's gonna tell me now
And I don't really care
No no no
I got a taste of paradise
That's all I really need to make me stay
I got a taste of paradise
If I had it any sooner you know
You know I never would have run away
  from my home

Heaven can wait
And all I got is time until the end of time
I won't look back
I won't look back
Let the altars shine

Heaven can wait
Heaven can wait
I won't look back
I won't look back
Let the altars shine
Let the altars shine

HEAVEN CAN WAIT

Words and Music by
JIM STEINMAN

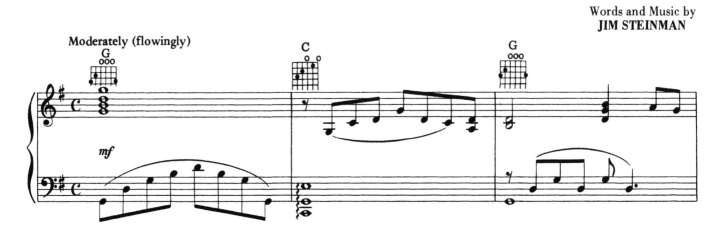

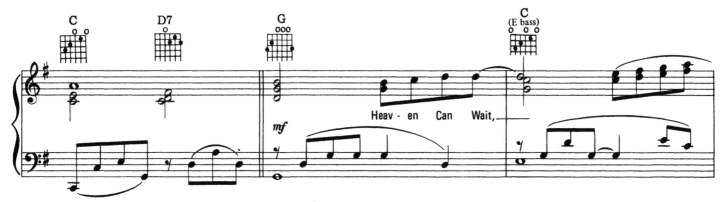

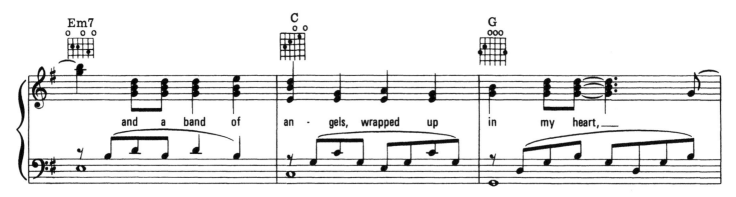

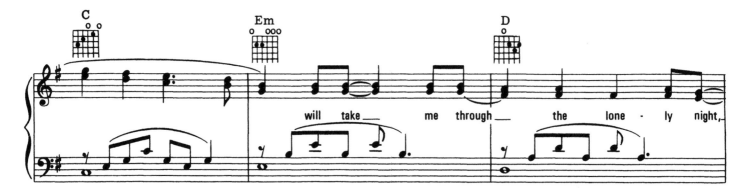

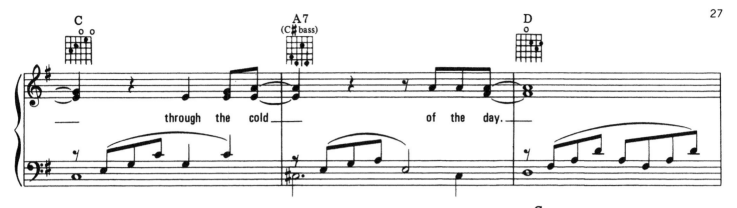

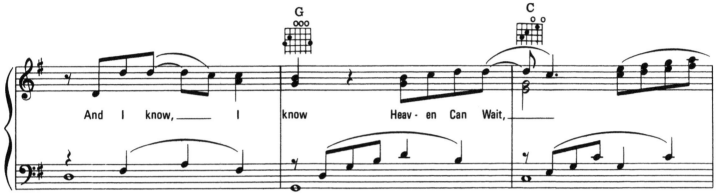

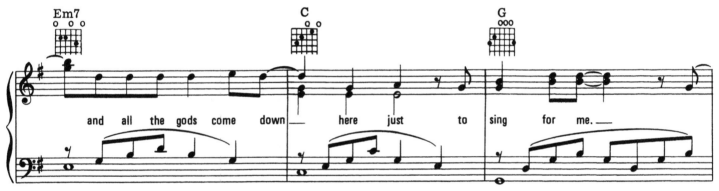

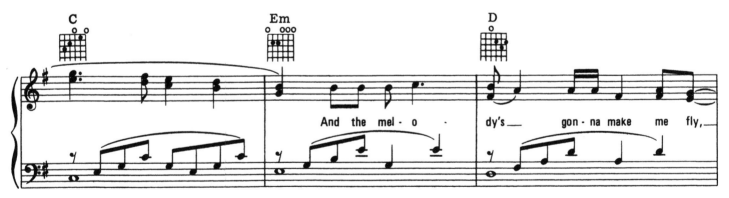

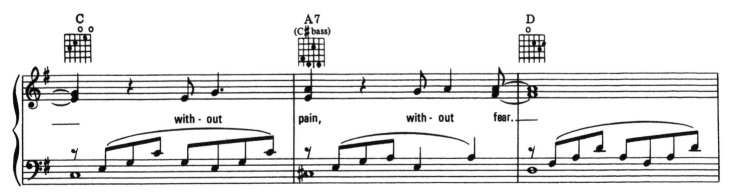

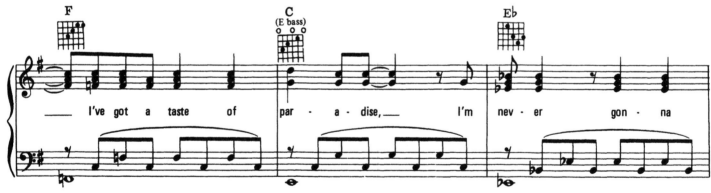

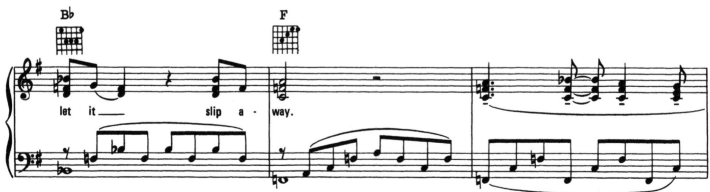

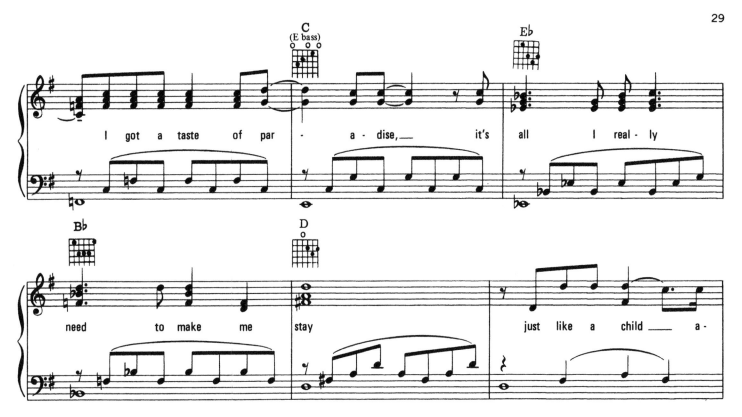

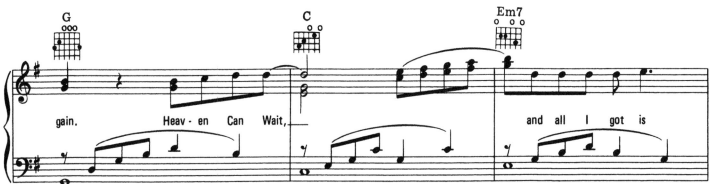

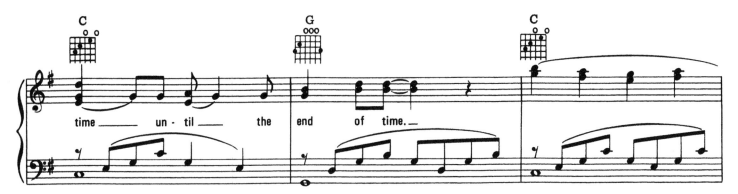

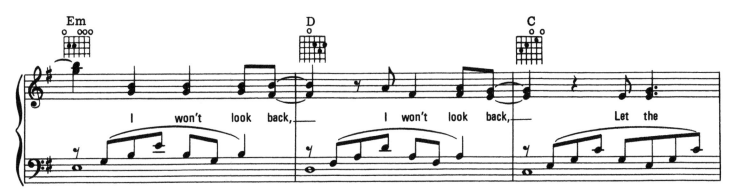

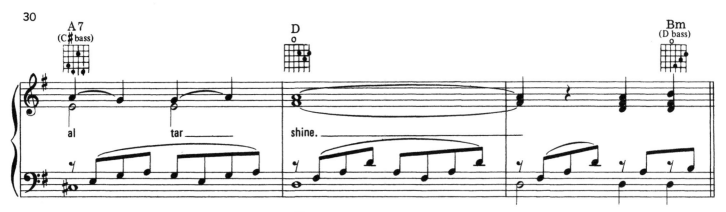

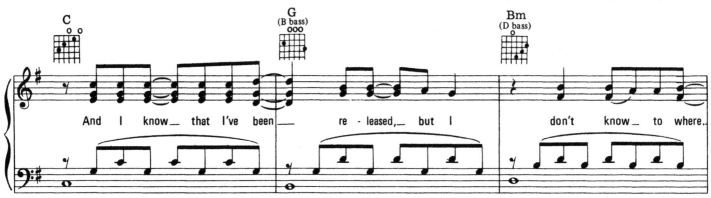

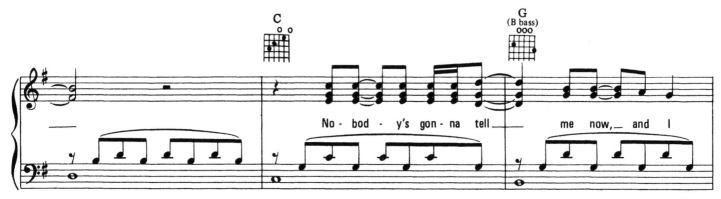

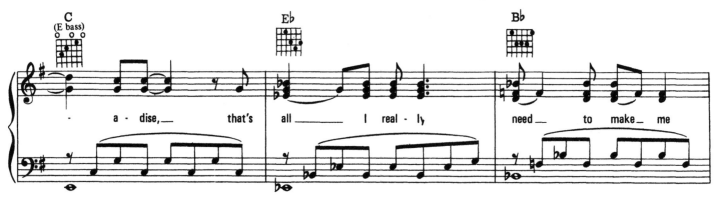

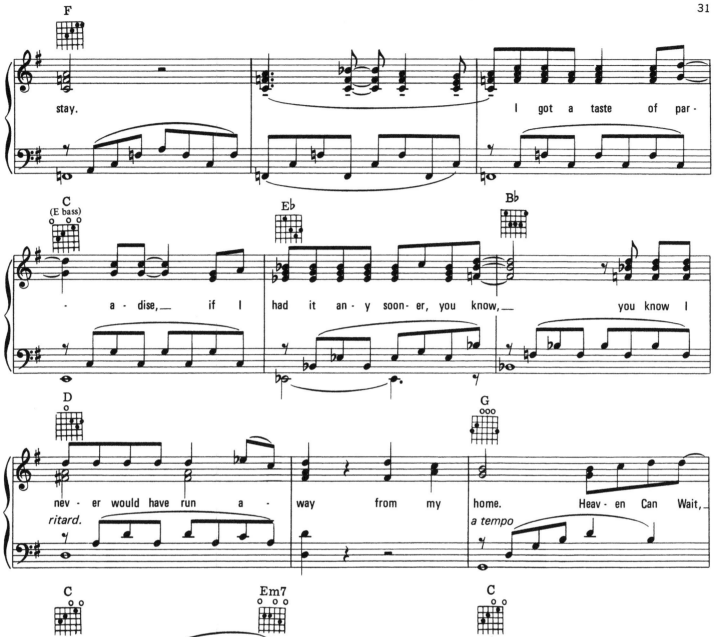

stay. I got a taste of par-

-a - dise,___ if I had it an - y soon - er, you know,___ you know I

ritard. nev - er would have run a - way from my home. *a tempo* Heav - en Can Wait,

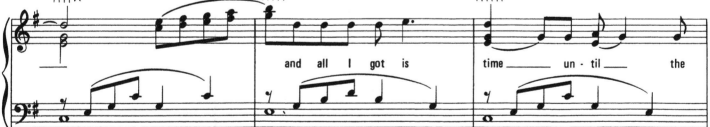

and all I got is time_____ un - til_____ the

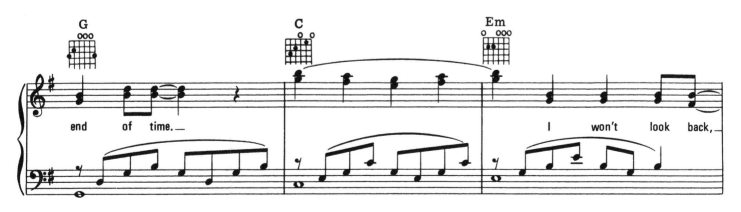

end of time.___ I won't look back,___

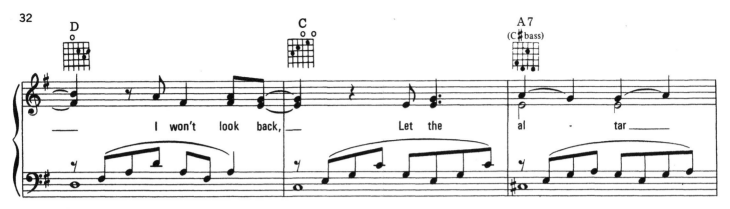

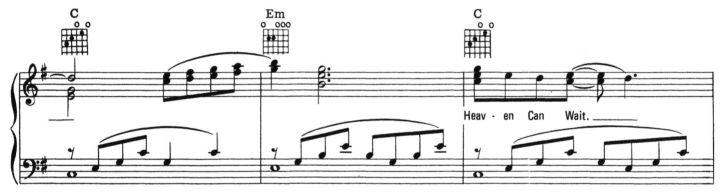

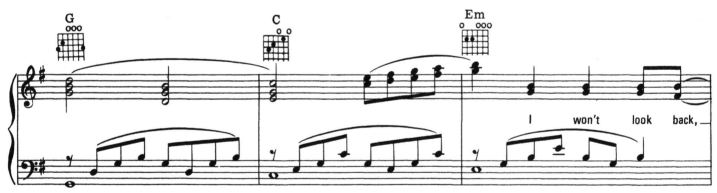

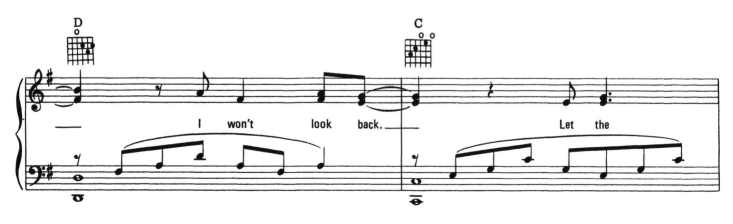

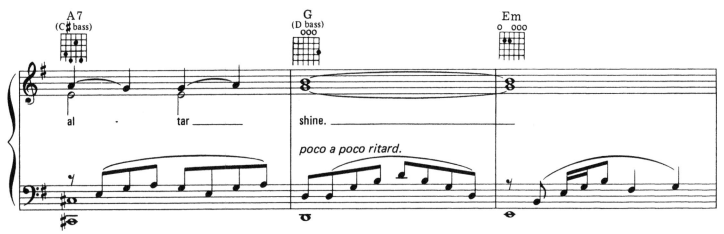

al - tar ___ shine. ___

poco a poco ritard.

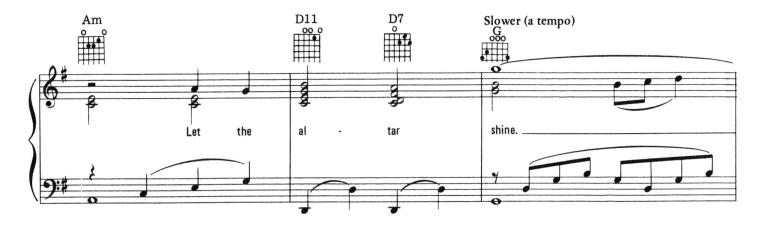

Let the al - tar shine. ___

Slower (a tempo)

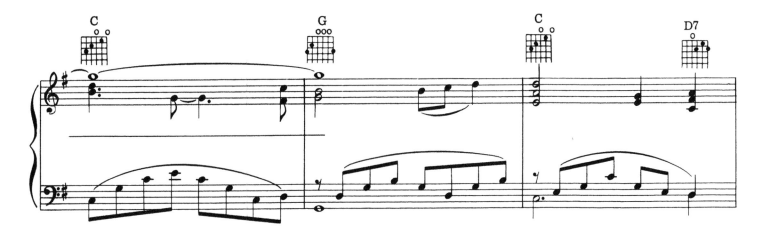

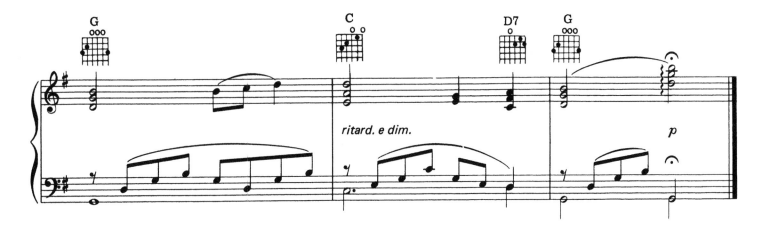

ritard. e dim.

p

ALL REVVED UP WITH NO PLACE TO GO

Words and Music by
JIM STEINMAN

I was nothing but a lonely boy
  looking for something new
And you were nothing but a lonely girl
But you were something
Something like a dream come true

I was a varsity tackle and a hell of a block
When I played my guitar
I made the canyons rock—but—
Every Saturday night
I felt the fever grow
Do ya know what it's like
All revved up with no place to go
Do ya know what it's like
All revved up with no place to go

In the middle of a steaming night
I'm tossing in my sleep
And in the middle of a red-eyed dream
I see you coming
Coming on to give it to me

I was out on the prowl down by the edge of the track
And like a son of a jackal
I'm a leader of the pack—but—
Every Saturday night
I felt the fever grow
Do ya know what it's like
All revved up with no place to go
Do ya know what it's like
All revved up with no place to go

Oh, Baby, I'm a hunter in the dark of the forest
I've been stalking you and tracking you down
Cruising up and down the main drag all night long
We could be standing at the top of the world
Instead of sinking further down in the mud
You and me 'round about midnight
You and me 'round about midnight
Someone's got to draw first

Draw first
Someone's got to draw first blood
Someone's got to draw first blood
Oooh I got to draw first blood
Oooh I got to draw first blood

I was out on the prowl down by the edge of the track—
And like a son of a jackal I'm a leader of the pack—but—
Every Saturday night
I felt the fever grow
Do ya know what it's like
All revved up with no place to go
Do ya know what it's like
All revved up with no place to go

I was nothing but a lonely all-American boy
Looking out for something to do
And you were nothing but a lonely all-American girl
But you were something like a dream come true
I was a varsity tackle and a hell of a block
And when I played my guitar I made the canyons rock
But every Saturday night
I felt the fever grow
All revved up with no place to go
All revved up with no place to go
All revved up with no place to go
All revved up with no place to go
All revved up with no place to go

ALL REVVED UP WITH NO PLACE TO GO

Words and Music by
JIM STEINMAN

MEAT LOAF & JIM STEINMAN

TWO OUT OF THREE AIN'T BAD

Words and Music by
JIM STEINMAN

Baby we can talk all night
But that ain't getting us nowhere .
I told you everything I possibly can
There's nothing left inside of here

And maybe you can cry all night
But that'll never change the way that I feel
The snow is really piling up outside
I wish you wouldn't make me leave here

I poured it on and I poured it out
I tried to show you just how much I care
I'm tired of words and I'm too hoarse to shout
But you've been cold to me so long
I'm crying icicles instead of tears

And all I can do is keep on telling you
I want you
I need you
But—there ain't no way I'm ever gonna love you
Now don't be sad
'Cause two out of three ain't bad
Now don't be sad
'Cause two out of three ain't bad

You'll never find your gold on a sandy beach
You'll never drill for oil on a city street
I know you're looking for a ruby in a mountain of rocks
But there ain't no Coupe de Ville hiding at the bottom
   of a Cracker Jack box

I can't lie
I can't tell you that I'm something I'm not
No matter how I try
I'll never be able
To give you something
Something that I just haven't got

There's only one girl that I will ever love
And that was so many years ago
And though I know I'll never get her out of my heart
She never loved me back
Ooh I know
I remember how she left me on a stormy night
She kissed me and got out of our bed
And though I pleaded and I begged her not to
   walk out that door
She packed her bags and turned right away

And she kept on telling me
She kept on telling me
She kept on telling me
I want you
I need you
But there ain't no way I'm ever gonna love you
Now don't be sad
'Cause two out of three ain't bad
I want you
I need you
But there ain't no way I'm ever gonna love you
Now don't be sad

'Cause two out of three ain't bad
Don't be sad
'Cause two out of three ain't bad

Baby we can talk all night
But that ain't getting us nowhere

TWO OUT OF THREE AIN'T BAD

Words and Music by
JIM STEINMAN

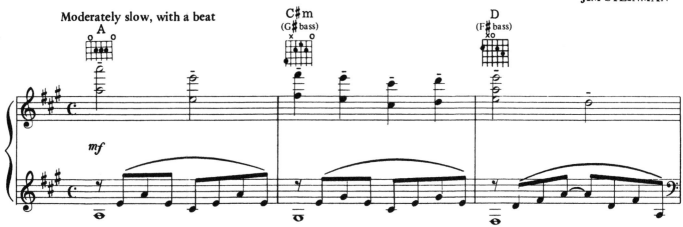

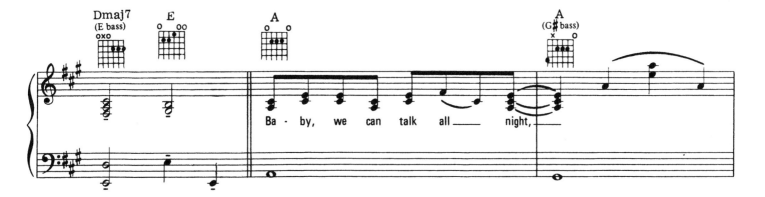

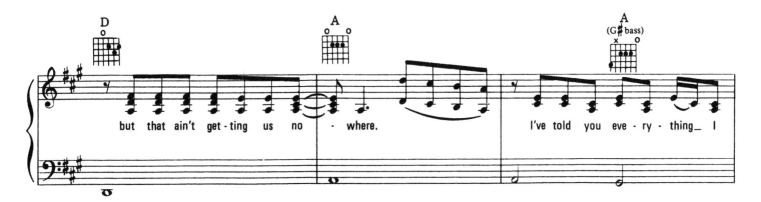

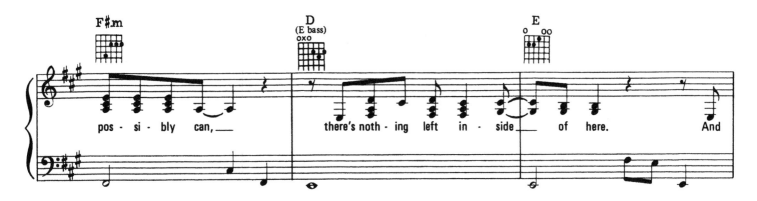

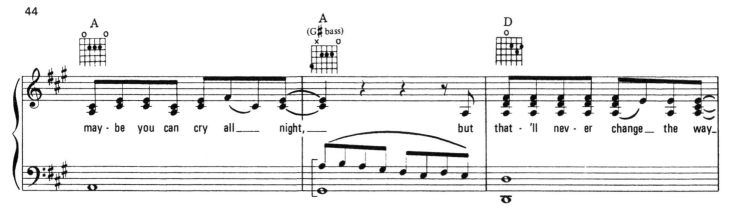

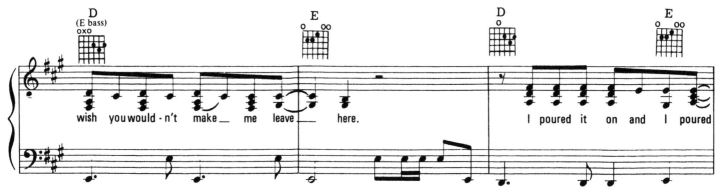

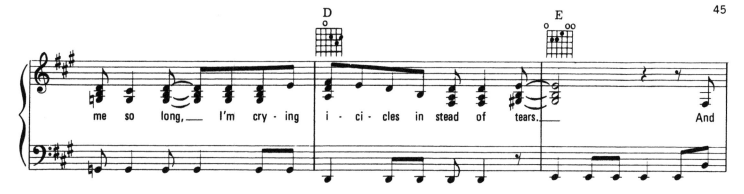

me so long,__ I'm cry-ing i-ci-cles in stead of tears.__ And

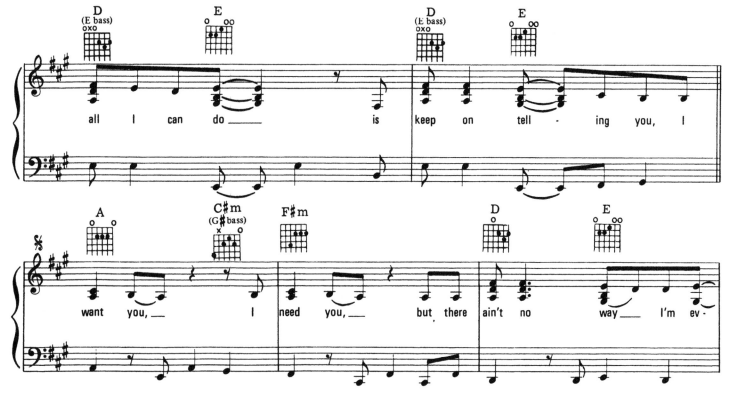

all I can do___ is keep on tell-ing you, I want you,__ I need you,__ but there ain't no way__ I'm ev-

-er gon-na love__ you, Now, don't be sad,__ (don't be sad) 'cause

Two Out Of Three__ Ain't__ Bad. Now don't be sad,__ 'cause

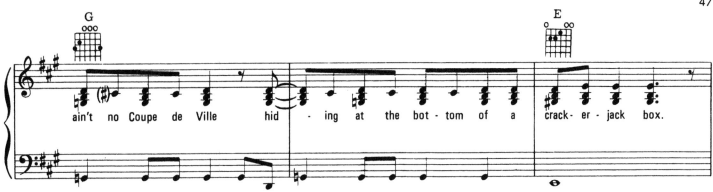

ain't no Coupe de Ville hid - ing at the bot - tom of a crack - er - jack box.

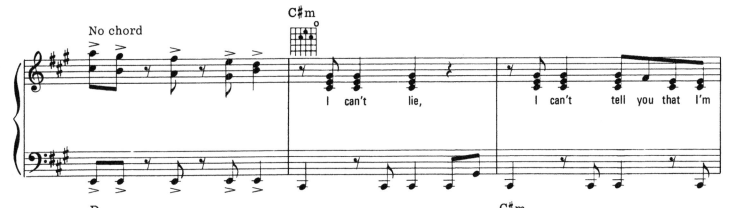

I can't lie, I can't tell you that I'm

some-thing I'm not, ___ no mat - ter how I try. I'll nev - er be a - ble

to give you some-thing, some-thing that I just have - n't got. ___ There's

on - ly one girl ___ that I will ev - er love, and that was so man - y years ___ a - go. ___

kept on tell - ing me, she kept on tell - ing me, she

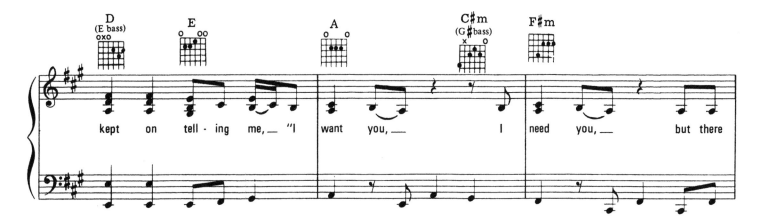

kept on tell - ing me, __ "I want you, __ I need you, __ but there

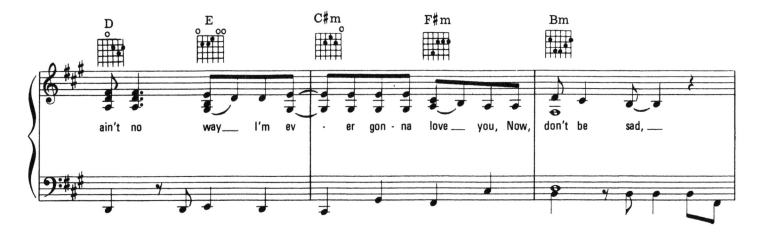

ain't no way __ I'm ev - er gon - na love __ you, Now, don't be sad, __

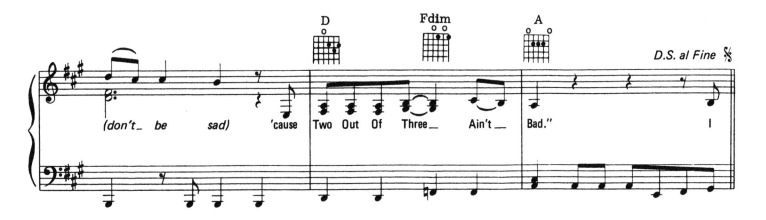

D.S. al Fine

(don't_ be sad) 'cause Two Out Of Three __ Ain't __ Bad." I

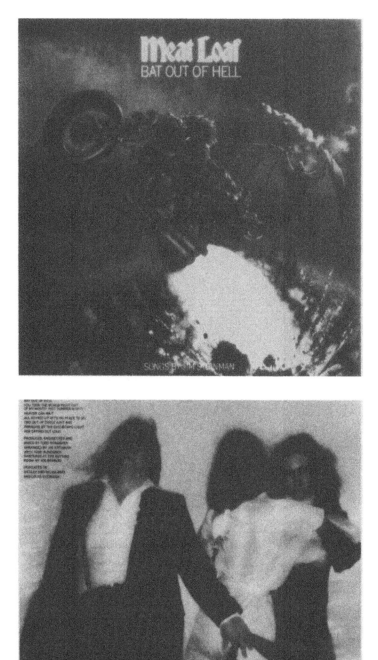

From beneath the grounds of a shrouded graveyard, a man on his motorcycle soars upward, shattering the face of his grave and breaking the barrier of his death. This illustration appears on the record cover of Meat Loaf's debut Cleveland International/epic album BAT OUT OF HELL and on this folio. Its power underscores the fruition of a joint musical venture that began three years ago.

Meat Loaf, besides possessing one of the world's great voices, is nobody to mess with. Born in Dallas, Texas into a family of southern gospel singers, Meat built a dynamic reputation 'gig drilling' with a west coast band. He was a lead singer with hard rock super-guitarist Ted Nugent on his album FREE FOR ALL, a gold and platinum record still on the charts. Meat Loaf recently portrayed the singing, crazy Eddie, a slick 50's leather-jacketed, grocery delivery boy in the Rocky Horror Picture Show. He's got deep roots in gospel and r & b and his ballads soar into the stratosphere, but the dark, burning heart at the center of this singing giant is always pumping out powerful rock and roll, thick, rich, explosive and hard, an outpouring so feverish and exciting, it would take a coronary bypass to stop it.

Jim Steinman, composer, arranger and pianist, grew up in the glazed and disoriented world of rock and roll 'midst the over-heated imagery of Claremont, California. Being abruptly removed to Long Island, he absorbed the best of two coasts of rock and roll. An avid practitioner of transcendental amnesia, he remembers nothing before the first golden moment he heard a Fender Telecaster overloading a Marshall amp.

Meat Loaf and Steinman joined forces in the National Lampoon Show. Their partnership flourished rapidly and within a year they were billed to perform at Carnegie Hall. Shortly after, together with producer Todd Rundgren, they recorded their sensational BAT OUT OF HELL album.

Full musical accord is evidently shared by the two partners in both thematic and stylistic interpretation. Both men are intensely romantic and their message is clear. Steinman's lyrics explore the many regions of man's desire, and Meat Loaf responds at gut level, echoing the changing shades of the love dream.

BAT OUT OF HELL continues to soar high!

PARADISE BY THE DASHBOARD LIGHT

Words and Music by **JIM STEINMAN**

I. Paradise

BOY: I remember every little thing
As if it happened only yesterday
Parking by the lake
And there was not another car in sight
And I never had a girl
Looking any better than you did
And all the kids at school
They were wishing they were me that night

And now our bodies are oh so close and tight
It never felt so good, it never felt so right
And we're glowing like the metal on the edge of a knife
Glowing like the metal on the edge of a knife
C'mon! Hold on tight!
C'mon! Hold on tight!

Though it's cold and lonely in the deep dark night
I can see paradise by the dashboard light

GIRL: Ain't no doubt about it
We were doubly blessed
Cause we were barely seventeen
And we were barely dressed

Ain't no doubt about it
Baby got to go and shout it
Ain't no doubt about it
We were doubly blessed

BOY: Cause we were barely seventeen
And we were barely dressed

Baby doncha hear my heart
You got it drowning out the radio
I've been waiting so long
For you to come along and have some fun

And I gotta let ya know
No you're never gonna regret it
So open up your eyes I got a big surprise
It'll feel all right
Well I wanna make your motor run

And now our bodies are oh so close and tight
It never felt so good, it never felt so right
And we're glowing like the metal on the edge of a knife
Glowing like the metal on the edge of a knife
C'mon! Hold on tight!
C'mon! Hold on tight!

Though it's cold and lonely in the deep dark night
I can see paradise by the dashboard light
Paradise by the dashboard light

You got to do what you can
And let Mother Nature do the rest
Ain't no doubt about it
We were doubly blessed
Cause we were barely seventeen
And we were barely—

We're gonna go all the way tonight
We're gonna go all the way
And tonight's the night . . . .

RADIO BROADCAST:
OK, here we go, we got a real pressure cooker
going here, two down, nobody on, no score,
bottom of the ninth, there's the wind-up, and
there it is, a line shot up the middle, look
at him go. This boy can really fly!
He's rounding first and really turning it on
now, he's not letting up at all, he's gonna
try for second; the ball is bobbled out in center,
and here comes the throw, and what a throw!
He's gonna slide in head first, here he comes, he's out!
No, wait, safe—safe at second base, this kid really
makes things happen out there.
Batter steps up to the plate, here's the pitch—
he's going, and what a jump he's got, he's trying
for third, here's the throw, it's in the dirt—
safe at third! Holy cow, stolen base!
He's taking a pretty big lead out there, almost
daring him to try and pick him off. The pitcher
glances over, winds up, and it's bunted, bunted
down the third base line, the suicide squeeze is on!
Here he comes, squeeze play, it's gonna be close,
here's the throw, here's the play at the plate,
holy cow, I think he's gonna make it!

II. Let Me Sleep On It

GIRL: Stop right there!
I gotta know right now!
Before we go any further—!

Do you love me?
Will you love me forever?
Do you need me?
Will you never leave me?
Will you make me so happy for the rest of my life?
Will you take me away and will you make me your wife?
Do you love me!?
Will you love me forever!?
Do you need me!?
Will you never leave me!?
Will you make me so happy for the rest of my life!?
Will you take me away and will you make me your wife!?
I gotta know right now
Before we go any further
Do you love me! ! ! ?
Will you love me forever ! ! ! ?

BOY: Let me sleep on it
Baby, baby let me sleep on it
Let me sleep on it
And I'll give you an answer in the morning

Let me sleep on it
Baby, baby let me sleep on it
Let me sleep on it
And I'll give you an answer in the morning

Let me sleep on it
Baby, baby let me sleep on it
Let me sleep on it
And I'll give you an answer in the morning

GIRL: I gotta know right now!
Do you love me?
Will you love me forever?
Do you need me?
Will you never leave me?
Will you make me so happy for the rest of my life?
Will you take me away and will you make me your wife?
I gotta know right now!
Before we go any further
Do you love me?
And will you love me forever?

BOY: Let me sleep on it
Baby, baby let me sleep on it
Let me sleep on it
And I'll give you an answer in the morning
Let me sleep on it! ! !

GIRL: Will you love me forever?

BOY: Let me sleep on it! ! !

GIRL: Will you love me forever! ! ! !

III. Praying for the End of Time

BOY: I couldn't take it any longer
Lord I was crazed
And when the feeling came upon me
Like a tidal wave
I started swearing to my god and on my mother's grave
That I would love you to the end of time
I swore that I would love you to the end of time!

So now I'm praying for the end of time
To hurry up and arrive
Cause if I gotta spend another minute with you
I don't think that I can really survive
I'll never break my promise or forget my vow
But God only knows what I can do right now
I'm praying for the end of time
It's all that I can do
Praying for the end of time, so I can end my time with you! ! !

BOY: It was long ago and it was far away
and it was so much better than it is today

GIRL: It never felt so good
It never felt so right
And we were glowing like
A metal on the edge of a knife

PARADISE BY THE DASHBOARD LIGHT

Words and Music by
JIM STEINMAN

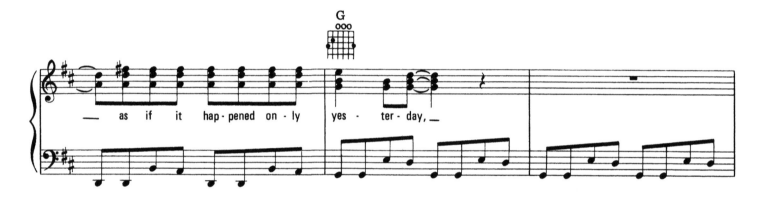

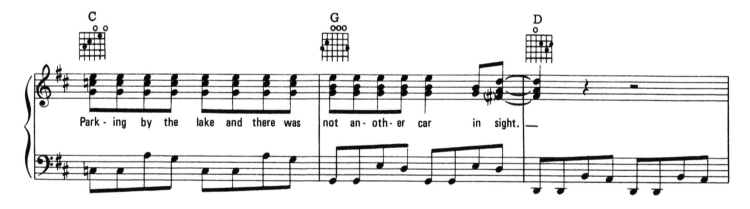

you did,　　　　　　　　　　And all the kids at school,＿ they were

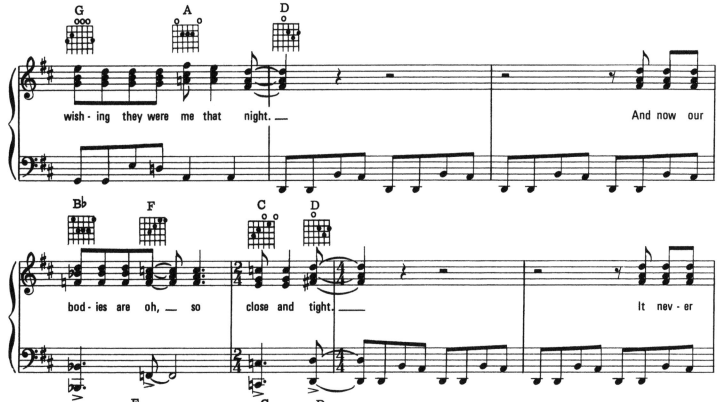

wish - ing they were me that night. ＿　　　　　　　　And now our

bod - ies are oh, ＿ so close and tight. ＿　　　　　　It nev - er

felt so good, ＿ it nev - er felt so right. ＿　　　　　And we're glow -

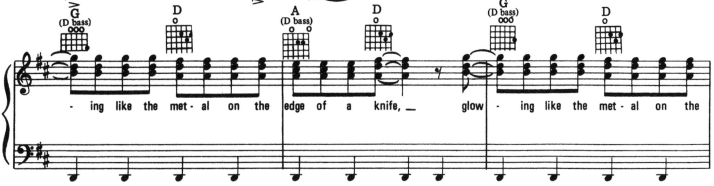

- ing like the met - al on the edge of a knife, ＿ glow - ing like the met - al on the

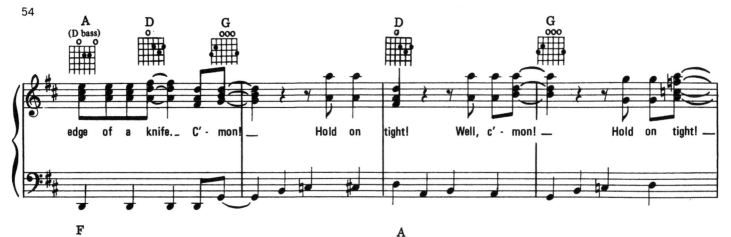

edge of a knife.__ C'-mon!__ Hold on tight! Well, c'-mon!__ Hold on tight!__

'Though it's

Moderately slow ($\quad = \quad$)

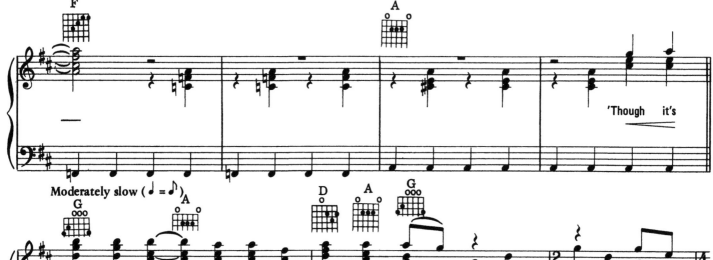

cold and lone-ly in the deep dark night,__ I can

see Par-a-dise__ By The Dash-board__ Light.

Moderately bright ($\quad = \quad$ as before), with a $\quad$ feel

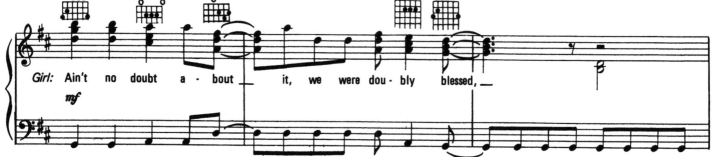

Girl: Ain't no doubt a-bout__ it, we were dou-bly blessed,__

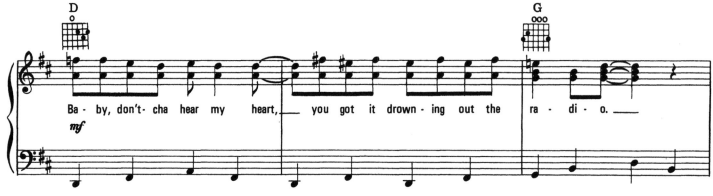

Ba - by, don't- cha hear my heart, you got it drown - ing out the ra - di - o.

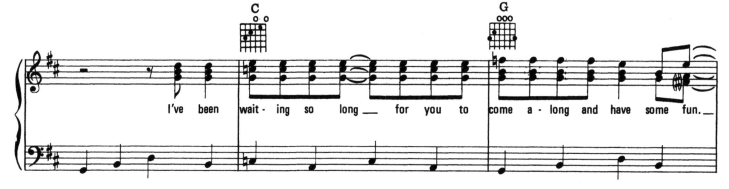

I've been wait - ing so long for you to come a - long and have some fun.

And I got - ta let ya know, no,

you're nev - er gon - na re - gret it. So o - pen

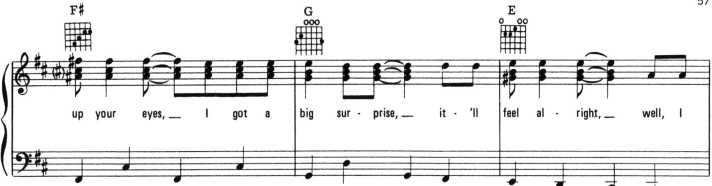

edge of a knife.__ C'-mon!__ Hold on tight! Well, c'-mon!__ Hold on tight.__

__ 'Though it's

Moderately slow (♩ = ♪)

cold and lone-ly in the deep dark night. I can

see Par-a-dise By__ The Dash-board Light.__ 'Though it's

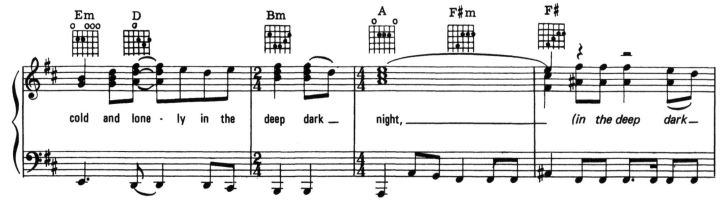

cold and lone-ly in the deep dark__ night,_____ *(in the deep dark__*

BASEBALL PLAY-BY-PLAY ON THE CAR RADIO

O.K., here we go, we got a real pressure cooker going here, two down, nobody on, no score, bottom of the ninth, there's the wind-up, and there it is, a line shot up the middle, look at him go. This boy can really fly!

He's rounding first and really turning it on now, he's not letting up at all, he's gonna try for second; the ball is bobbled out in center, and here comes the throw, and what a throw! He's gonna slide in head first, here he comes, he's out! No, wait safe,—safe at second base, this kid really makes things happen out there.

Batter steps up to the plate, here's the pitch—he's going, and what a jump he's got, he's trying for third, here's the throw, it's in the dirt,—safe at third! Holy cow, stolen base!

He's taking a pretty big lead out there, almost daring him to try and pick him off. The pitcher glances over, winds up, and it's bunted, bunted down the third base line, the suicide squeeze is on! Here he comes, squeeze play, it's gonna be close, here's the throw, here's the play at the plate, holy cow, I think he's gonna make it!

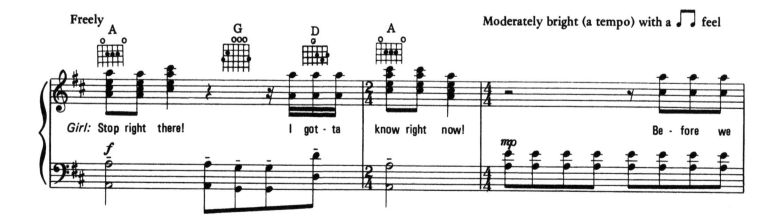

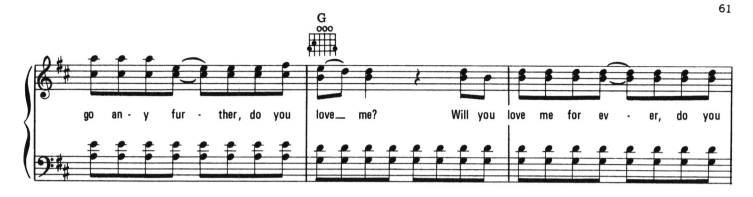

go an - y fur - ther, do you love__ me? Will you love me for ev - er, do you

need me? Will you nev - er leave __ me? Will you make me so hap - py for the

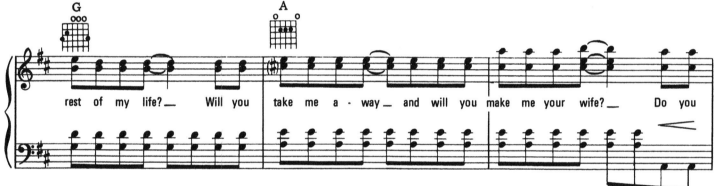

rest of my life?__ Will you take me a - way__ and will you make me your wife?__ Do you

love me? Will you love me for - ev - er? Do you need __ me? Will you

nev - er leave __ me? Will you make me so hap - py for the rest of my life?__ Will you

take me a - way ___ and will you make me your wife? ___ I got - ta know right now,

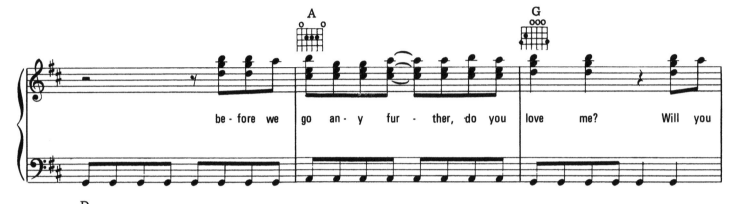

be - fore we go an - y fur - ther, do you love me? Will you

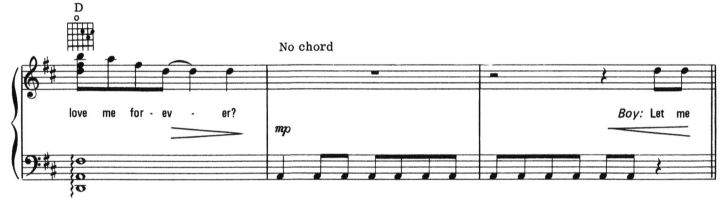

love me for - ev - er? *mp* *Boy:* Let me

sleep on ___ it. ___ *mf* Ba - by, ba - by, let me sleep on it. ___

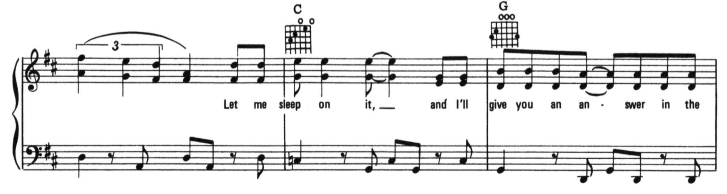

Let me sleep on it, ___ and I'll give you an an - swer in the

morn - ing. Let me sleep on _ it. _

Ba - by, ba - by, let me sleep on it. _ Let me sleep on it. _ I'll

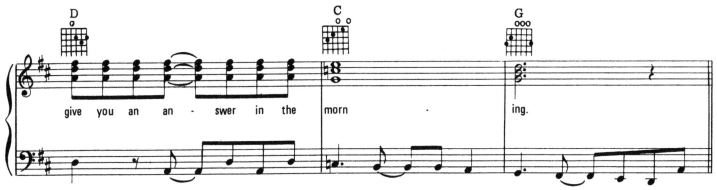

give you an an - swer in the morn - ing.

poco a poco cresc.

Girl: I got - ta know right now! Do you love me? Will you

love me for - ev - er? Do you need me? Will you nev - er leave _ me? Will you

make me so hap-py for the rest of my life?___ Will you take me a-way___ and will you

make me your wife?___ I got-ta know right now! Be-fore we

go an-y fur-ther, do you love me? Will you love me for-ev-er?

No chord

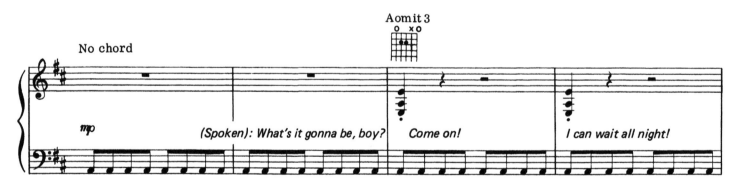

(Spoken): What's it gonna be, boy? Come on! I can wait all night!

No chord

What's it gonna be, boy... yes or no? What's it gonna be, boy? Yes...

or . . . no? *Boy (sung):* Let me sleep on____ it.____

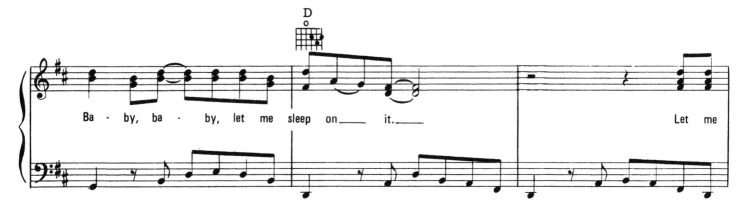

Ba - by, ba - by, let me sleep on____ it.____ Let me

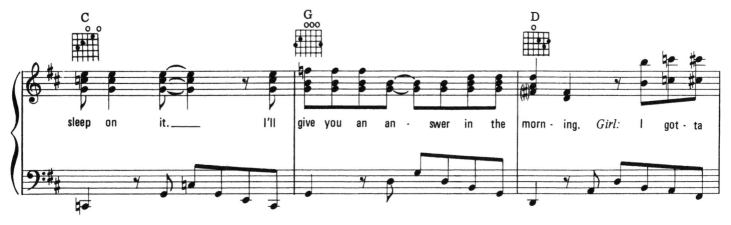

sleep on it.____ I'll give you an an - swer in the morn - ing. *Girl:* I got - ta

Boy obbligato:

Let me sleep on____ it.____ Ba - by, ba - by, let me

know right now! Do you love me? Will you love me for ev - er? Do you

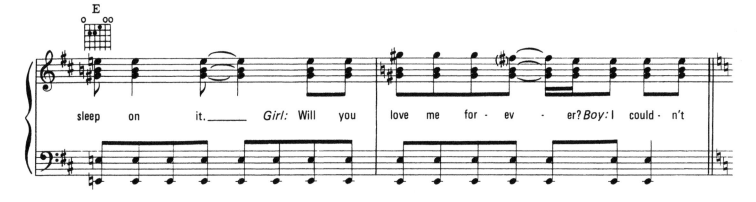

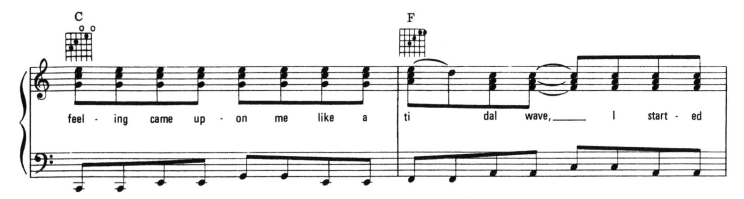

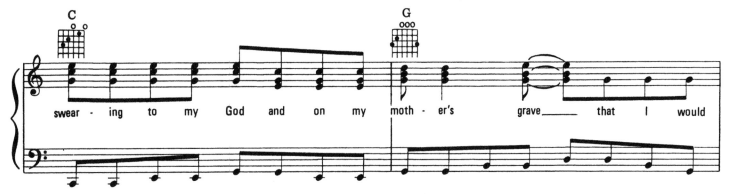

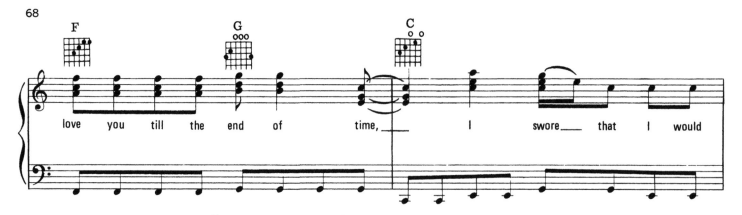

love you till the end of time,   I swore___ that I would

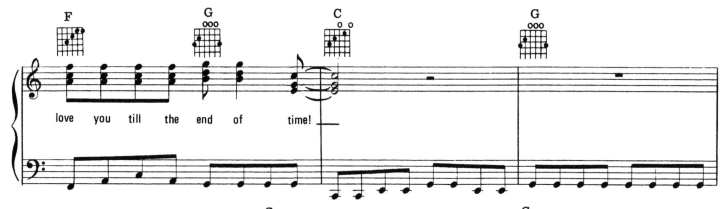

love you till the end of time!

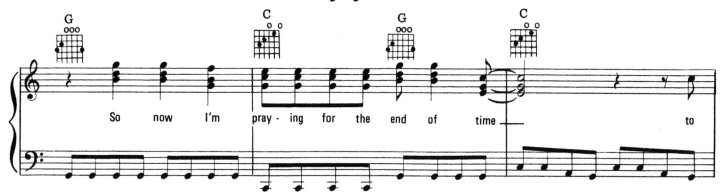

So now I'm pray-ing for the end of time ___ to

hur-ry up and ar-rive. ___ 'Cause

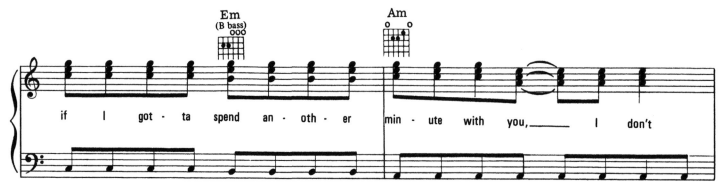

if I got-ta spend an-oth-er min-ute with you, ___ I don't

think that I can real - ly sur - vive. _____ I'll nev - er

break my prom - ise or for - get my vow, _____ But

God on - ly knows _____ what I can do right now. I'm

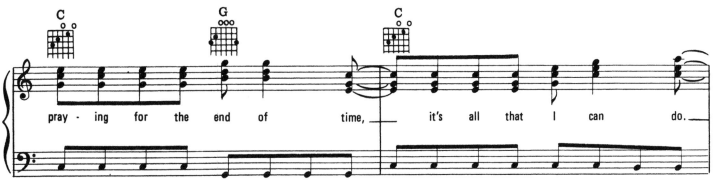

pray - ing for the end of time, _____ it's all that I can do. _____

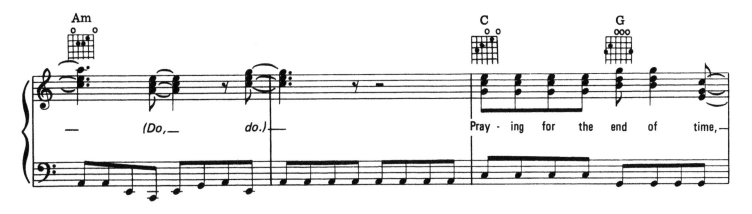

_____ (Do, _____ do.) _____ Pray - ing for the end of time, _____

FOR CRYING OUT LOUD

Words and Music by
JIM STEINMAN

I was lost till you were found
But I never knew how far down
I was falling
Before I reached the bottom

I was cold and you were fire
And I never knew how the pyre
Could be burning
On the edge of the ice field

And now the chilly California wind
Is blowing down our bodies again
And we're sinking deeper and deeper in the
  chilly California sand
Oh I know you belong inside my aching heart
And can't you see my faded Levis bursting apart
And don't you hear me crying:
"Oh Babe, don't go"
And don't you hear me screaming:
"How was I to know?"

I'm in the middle of nowhere
Near the end of the line
But there's a border to somewhere waiting
And there's a tankful of time
Oh give me just another moment to see the light of the day
And take me to another land where I don't have to stay
And I'm gonna need somebody to make me feel like you do
And I will receive somebody with open arms, open eyes,
Open up the sky and let the planet that I love shine through

For crying out loud
You know I love you
For crying out loud
You know I love you
For crying out loud
You know I love you

I was damned and you were saved
And I never knew how enslaved
I was kneeling
In the chains of my master

I could laugh but you could cry
And I never knew just how high
I was flying
Ah, with you right above me

And now the chilly California wind
Is blowing down our bodies again
And we're sinking deeper and deeper in the
  chilly California sand
Oh I know you belong inside my aching heart
And can't you see my faded Levis bursting apart
And don't you hear me crying:
"Oh Babe, don't go"
And don't you hear me screaming:
"How was I to know?"

I'm in the middle of nowhere
Near the end of the line
But there's a border to somewhere waiting
And there's a tankful of time
Oh give me just another moment to see the light of the day
And take me to another land where I don't have to stay
And I'm gonna need somebody to make me feel like you do
And I will receive somebody with open arms, open eyes,
Open up the sky and let the planet that I love shine through

For crying out loud
You know I love you
For crying out loud
You know I love you
For crying out loud
You know I love you

For taking in the rain when I'm feeling so dry
For giving me the answers when I'm asking you why
My oh my
For that I thank you

For taking in the sun when I'm feeling so cold
For giving me a child when my body is old
Don't you know
For that I need you

For coming to my room when you know I'm alone
For finding me a highway and for driving me home
You got to know
For that I serve you

For pulling me away when I'm starting to fall
For revving me up when I'm starting to stall
And all in all
For that I want you

For taking and for giving and for playing the game
For praying for my future in the days that remain
Oh Lord
For that I hold you

Ah, but most of all
For crying out loud
For that I love you
Ah, but most of all
For crying out loud
For that I love you
Ah, but most of all
For crying out loud
For that I love you

When you're crying out loud
You know I love you

FOR CRYING OUT LOUD

Words and Music by
JIM STEINMAN

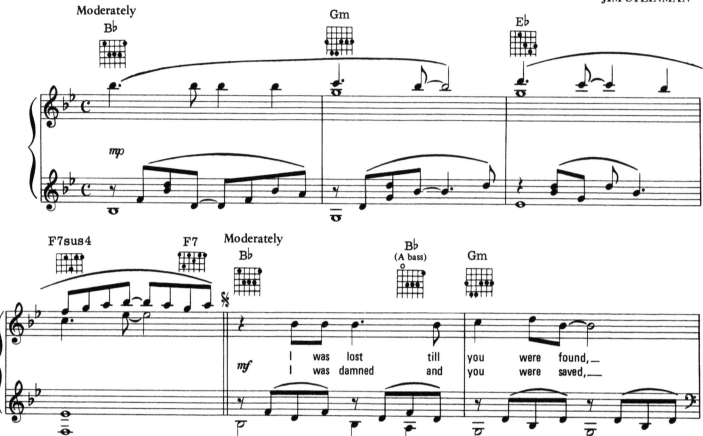

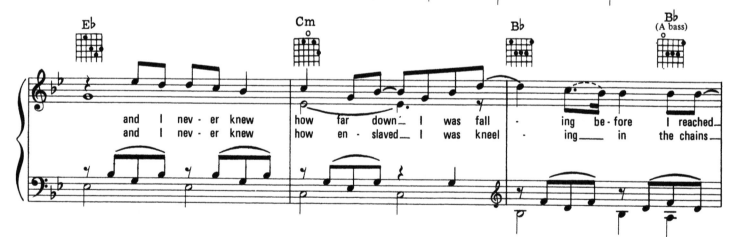

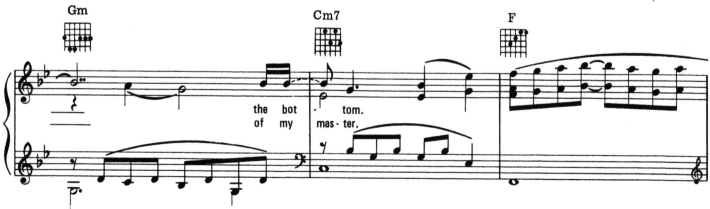

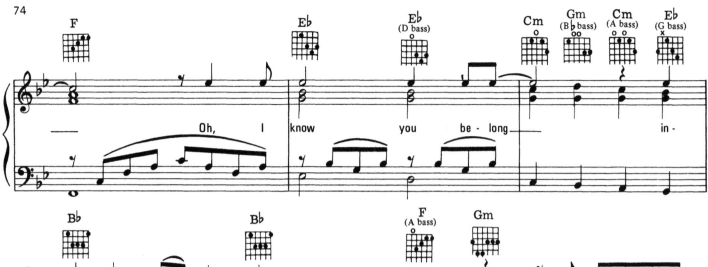

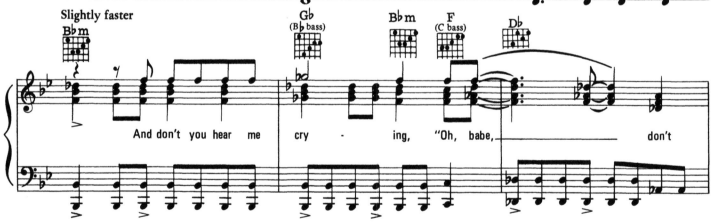

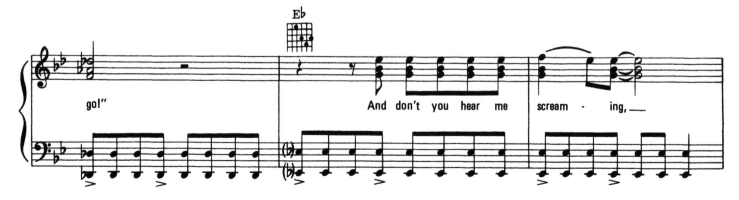

"How was I to know?" *poco a poco cresc.*

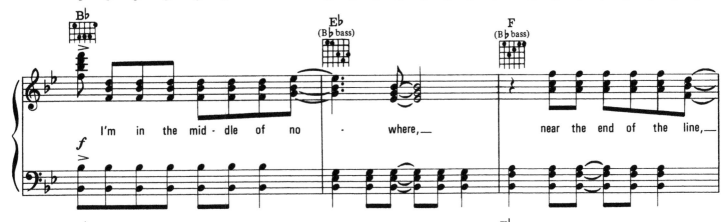

I'm in the mid - dle of no - where, __ near the end of the line, __

f

But there's a bor - der to some - where wait - ing, __

and there's a tank - ful of time. Oh, give me just an -

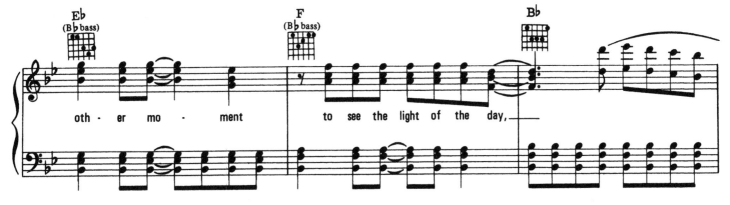

oth - er mo - ment to see the light of the day, __

Oh, For Cry - ing Out Loud,___ you know I love you.___

rall. For Cry - ing Out Loud, you know I love you... For

tak - ing in the rain when I'm feel - ing so dry, For giv - ing me the an - swers when I'm
com - ing to my room when you know I'm a lone, For find - ing me a high - way, for

ask - ing you why, And my, oh my,___ for that I thank_you.
driv - ing me home, And you gotta know,___ for that I serve_you.

For tak - ing in the sun when I'm feel - ing so cold, For
For pull - ing me a - way when I'm start - ing to fall, For

giv - ing me a child when my bod - y is old, ___ And don't you
rev - ving me up ___ when I'm start - ing to stall, ___ And all in

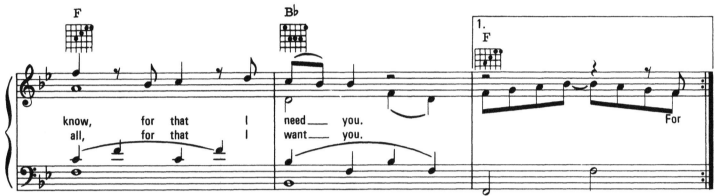

know, for that I need ___ you.
all, for that I want ___ you. For

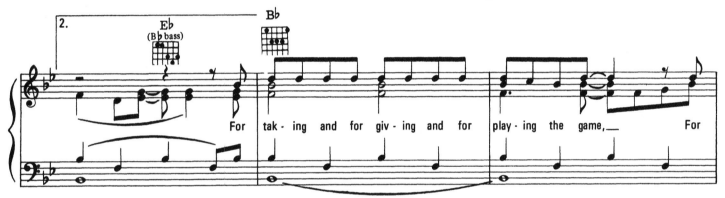

For tak - ing and for giv - ing and for play - ing the game, ___ For

pray - ing for my fu - ture in the days that re - main. ___ Oh, ___

Lord, ___ for that I hold you. Ah, but most ___ of all, ___

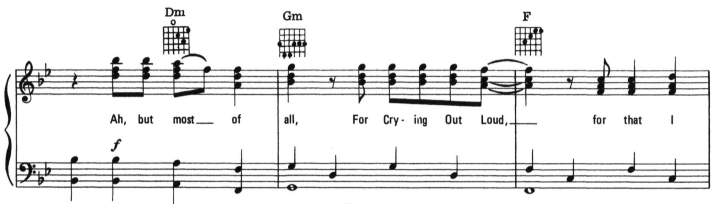

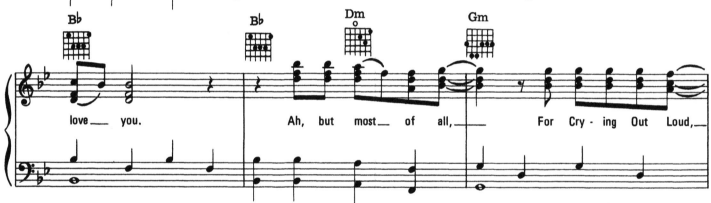

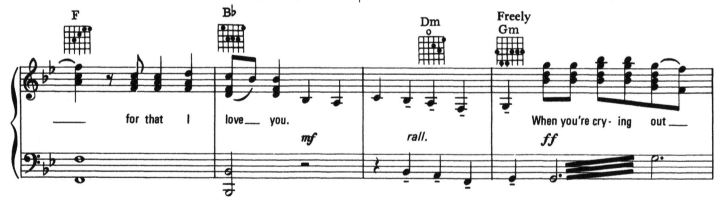

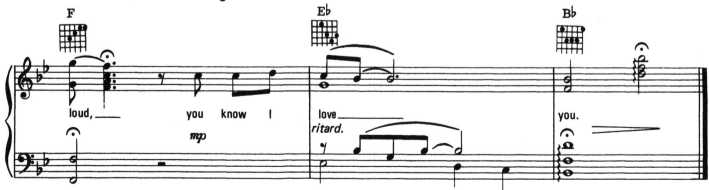